Introduction

Apart from that 'extra special taste', one of the great delights of home baking is the evocative aroma that permeates a whole building – be it croft or castle – when the cakes or scones come off the girdle. The tradition of home baking goes back many centuries in Scotland, from the time that oatcakes, bannocks and scones were made easily and quickly over an open fire on a girdle – that simplest but most versatile piece of kitchen equipment. Inside or out, by this method baking was quick and without fuss.

By the nineteenth century, equipment and methods, as well as ingredients, had become more sophisticated. Scottish bakers in crofts and castles rose quickly to the challenge. Many modern housewives, of course, would rather make a quick trip to a local supermarket to buy pre-packed cakes which, while of excellent quality, lack that mystic dimension of the home-made product.

For the past twelve years at Brodick Castle, on the lovely Scottish Island of Arran, the National Trust for Scotland have been fortunate in having the services of a fuineadair *(Gaelic for baker) of extraordinary ability. She is seventy-six-year-old Mrs Anna McCabe who, single-handed, bakes each year for over 50,000 visitors who come across the Firth of Clyde to visit one of Scotland's finest castles and its superb gardens.*

Born in Ayr in 1907, Anna McCabe began her working life in a factory. But, before she turned twenty, the call of her mother's bakery business in Glasgow proved too strong to resist. She went there and quickly learnt the art of baking from her sister, Everett, some twelve years her senior. A few years later the family emigrated to America, but Anna married a Glasgow man and remained in Scotland.

After she had brought up her own family, she and her husband were involved in various catering enterprises until 1973, when she came to Brodick to be the sole occupant and uncrowned queen of the castle bakehouse. Her fame is such that one journalist came specially from France not to view the magnificent treasures of the castle but to savour Mrs McCabe's unrivalled apple tarts. Readers may themselves acquire some of her skills by a careful study of this book.

John M. Forgie
Former Administrator, Brodick Castle.

Left: **Brodick Castle on the Isle of Arran**

Loch Tummel, Tayside

Kyleakin Harbour, Skye

Almond Strips

2 egg whites, 3 oz caster sugar
3 oz ground almonds, Raspberry or strawberry jam
6 oz plain flour, 3 oz margarine
Flaked almonds

Make pastry, using 6 oz flour and 3 oz margarine.
Line a swiss roll tin with the pastry and spread evenly
with jam. Whisk the egg whites until stiff, then fold in
sugar and almonds. Spread this mixture on top of the
jam in the case, and sprinkle with flaked almonds. Bake
in centre of oven, preheated to 350°F, 180°C, gas
mark 4, for 30 minutes or until brown. Cut into fingers
when hot.

Makes 12 pieces

Note: Individual ovens may be hotter or cooler than
the 'average' when at any given setting. For this
reason, it is wise to keep an eye on the contents of
your oven towards the end of the baking time shown
in each recipe, as the actual cooking time needed may
be a little shorter or longer than that shown.

Ayrshire Pancakes

*10 oz self-raising flour, 3 oz caster sugar, 3 size 3 eggs
1 dsp hot oil, $\frac{1}{4}$ pt milk and $\frac{1}{4}$ pt water mixed*

*Place flour in a bowl and make a well in the centre. Crack the
eggs into a cup, then pour into the well with the sugar.
Gradually combine the eggs and sugar with the flour, working
from the centre outwards and bringing in the flour a little at a
time. Then add half the milk and water and beat mixture until
smooth. Add enough of the remaining liquid to make a thick
batter, then beat in the hot oil. Heat a thick based large frying
pan, girdle or iron grill plate to a fairly hot temperature and
brush lightly with oil. Drop tablespoonfuls of the mixture on
to the pan, and turn when bubbles rise to the surface. Keep
earlier batches warm in a folded tea-towel until all the
pancakes are cooked.*

Makes 20 pancakes

Bakehouse Scones

10 oz self-raising flour
4 oz margarine, 3 oz sugar, $\frac{1}{4}$ pt milk

*Place the flour in a bowl and make a well in the centre.
Put the sugar and margarine in the centre of the well,
then gradually combine ingredients by working from the
centre outwards and bringing in the flour a little at a
time. Add enough milk to make a soft dough. Roll out
on a floured board to $\frac{1}{2}-\frac{3}{4}$ in. thickness, then cut into
rounds with a 3 in. cutter. Bake in a moderate oven,
350°F, 180°C, gas mark 4, for 10–15 minutes.*

Makes 12 scones

Brathwick Shortbread

8 oz softened butter
4 oz caster sugar, 1 lb plain flour

Place butter, flour and sugar together in a bowl and, using one hand, squeeze the ingredients together until a cohesive ball of dough forms. Alternatively, place butter and sugar in the bowl of a mixer and mix together but do not mix to a cream. Add flour at a slow speed until a dough forms that can be handled. Divide the ball of dough into three, and either press each third into a shortbread mould or roll each out to a round about 7 in. across. Place each moulded or rolled out round on to a baking sheet and bake in the centre of a preheated oven, 325°F, 160°C, gas mark 3, for 25–30 minutes or until lightly browned. Whilst warm cut each into eight pieces.

Makes 3 rounds (24 pieces)

Brodick Castle Rock Cakes

8 oz self-raising flour, 4 oz margarine
4 oz caster sugar, 3 oz currants
1 size 3 egg, Milk to mix

Place flour, margarine, sugar and egg in a bowl and mix together until well blended. Add a little milk to make a stiff dough, then add currants. Drop spoonfuls of the mixture in heaps on a greased baking sheet, allowing them room to spread a little. Bake in the centre of a moderate oven, 350°F, 180°C, gas mark 4, for 15–20 minutes or until golden brown. Sprinkle with caster sugar when warm, if liked, and cool on a wire rack

Makes 12–15 buns

Tongue Bay, Highland

Blackrock Cottage, Glencoe, Highland

Ramsay Lane, Edinburgh

Dryburgh Abbey, Borders

Butterfly Cakes

10 oz self-raising flour
6 oz caster sugar, 6 oz margarine
4 size 3 eggs, 6 oz icing sugar
2 oz butter, Vanilla essence

Cream margarine and sugar together until the mixture is light and fluffy. Beat in eggs, one at a time, then fold in the flour. Fill 12 paper cake cases with the mixture and bake in the centre of a moderate oven, 350°F, 180°C, gas mark 4, for 15–20 minutes, or until tops of cakes spring back when pressed lightly. Cool on a wire rack. Make buttercream by combining icing sugar and softened butter and adding a few drops of vanilla essence to flavour. Cut tops off cooled cakes, place a

spoonful of buttercream on each, then replace tops, cutting them in half and inserting the two pieces at an angle into the buttercream to represent wings. Dust lightly with icing sugar if liked.

N.B. This mixture can also be used to make a sponge round: grease and bottom-line a 2 in. deep, 7 in. diameter sandwich tin, spread mixture evenly in tin and bake for 30–35 minutes at the same temperature as for the butterfly cakes. Cool on a wire rack, split in half and sandwich together with jam.

For a chocolate sponge, proceed in the same way but replace 2 oz of flour with 2 oz cocoa. Sandwich together with chocolate buttercream when cool.

Castle Butter Fingers

6 oz butter or margarine, 4 oz caster sugar
6 oz self-raising flour, 4 oz desiccated coconut
2 oz cocoa, 4 oz plain chocolate cake covering

Place butter or margarine, sugar and cocoa in a bowl
and cream well together until light and fluffy. Fold in
the flour and the desiccated coconut (the mixture will be
very stiff, but keep mixing until the ingredients are
well amalgamated). Grease a 7 × 11 in. sandwich tin
and press the mixture into it, being careful to make an
even layer and pressing it well into the corners. Bake in
the centre of a preheated oven, 350°F, 180°C, gas mark
4, for 30 minutes. When cool, cover with chocolate cake
covering, following the directions for melting given on
the packet, and cut into fingers.

Makes 20 pieces

Celtic Cakes

6 oz caster sugar, 2 oz margarine
6 oz ground rice, 3 size 3 eggs
Raspberry or strawberry jam
Pastry: 6 oz plain flour, 3 oz margarine

Make pastry using 6 oz flour and 3 oz margarine. Line the sections of a 16-bun tin with pastry and place a little jam in each case. Cream together margarine and sugar, then add eggs one at a time, beating well after each addition. Fold in the ground rice. Fill the pastry cases with this mixture, then place two strips of pastry cross-wise on top of each cake. Bake in the centre of a moderate oven, 350°F, 180°C, gas mark 4, for 25–30 minutes. Cool on a wire rack.

Makes 16 cakes

Kenmore Bridge, Loch Tay, Highland

Loch Eil, Highland

Loch Carron, Highland

Ardivachair Point, South Uist, Western Isles

Cladach Mince Pies

6 oz plain flour, 3 oz margarine
Mincemeat, Icing sugar

Make pastry using 6 oz flour and 3 oz margarine. Roll out thinly and use to line the sections of a 16-bun tin. Place a teaspoon of mincemeat in each case, then bake the pies in a moderate oven, 350°F, 180°C, gas mark 4, for about 20 minutes or until pastry is golden. Cool on a wire rack, then ice with water icing (mix icing sugar with hot water until a runny paste is formed, then place a teaspoonful on each pie and leave to set).

Makes 16 pies

Country Coconut Cakes

4 oz desiccated coconut, 2 oz caster sugar
2 size 3 eggs, Milk (if needed)
6 oz plain flour, 3 oz margarine
Raspberry or strawberry jam, Glacé cherries

Make pastry using 6 oz flour and 3 oz margarine. Line
the sections of a 12-bun tin with pastry and place a little
jam in each case. Mix together the coconut, sugar and
eggs, adding a little milk if the mixture is very dry. Fill
the cases with this mixture and place half a glacé cherry
on top of each cake. Bake in an oven preheated to
375°F, 190°C, gas mark 5, for 25–30 minutes or until
browned. Cool on a wire rack.

Makes 12 cakes

Duchess of Montrose Squares

2 egg whites, 3 oz caster sugar
3 oz ground almonds, Raspberry or strawberry jam
Mincemeat, 8 oz plain flour, 4 oz margarine

Make pastry using 8 oz flour and 4 oz margarine. Line
a deep swiss roll tin with the pastry, and spread base of
pastry evenly with jam. Cover jam with a layer of
mincemeat. Whisk the egg whites until stiff, then fold
in the sugar and almonds. Spread this macaroon mixture
over the mincemeat, then bake in the centre of a
preheated oven, 350°F, 180°C, gas mark 4, for 35–45
minutes. Dust with caster sugar, if liked, and cut
when hot.

Makes 12 squares

Duke's Fruit Cake

12 oz currants, 2 oz caster sugar, Boiling water
2 tsps mixed spice, 12 oz plain flour, 6 oz margarine

*Pour boiling water over the currants to cover, and allow
to stand for quarter of an hour. Meanwhile, make
shortcrust pastry using 12 oz flour and 6 oz margarine.
Line a 7 × 11 in. swiss roll tin with just over half the
pastry. Strain off the water from the currants and mix
the spice and sugar into the fruit. Spoon this mixture
evenly into the lined tin, then top with remaining
pastry. Bake in the centre of the oven, preheated to a
temperature of 375°F, 190°C, gas mark 5, for
30 minutes. Cut into 12 squares when still warm.*

Makes 12 squares

Brig o' Doon, Alloway, Strathclyde

Sunset over the Isle of Skye

Edinburgh Castle

Loch Awe, Strathclyde

Macaroon Tarts

2 egg whites, 3 oz caster sugar
3 oz ground almonds, Flaked almonds
6 oz plain flour, 3 oz margarine

*Make pastry, using 6 oz flour and 3 oz margarine.
Line the sections of a 12-bun tin with pastry. Whisk
the egg whites until stiff, then fold in the sugar and
almonds. Fill pastry cases with the mixture and scatter a
few flaked almonds on the top of each tart. Bake in a
slow oven, 325°F, 160°C, gas mark 3, for 35–45
minutes. Cool on a wire rack.*

Makes 12 tarts

Meringue Delights

4 egg whites, 12 oz caster sugar
1 level tsp baking powder, Whipped cream to fill
Glacé cherries to decorate

Beat all the ingredients together until mixture is very
stiff. Pipe on to a baking tray lined with greaseproof
paper. Bake in a very cool oven, 275°F, 140°C, gas
mark 1, for 1 hour. Makes 24 shells which may be
doubled up with cream and cherry topping.

Makes 24 meringues

Scottish Dainties

1 lb margarine, 4 oz icing sugar, 1 size 3 egg, 1 lb plain flour
Buttercream: 6 oz icing sugar, 2 oz butter, 4 oz chocolate

Cream margarine and sugar together until soft and fluffy. Beat in the egg, then add the flour gradually until all is combined into the mixture. Grease three baking sheets, then, using a large star tube, pipe the mixture on to the trays, making 36 biscuit shapes. Bake in a hot oven, 400°F, 200°C, gas mark 6, for 10–15 minutes, keeping a close eye on them to see that they do not brown too quickly. Cool on wire racks, then dip half of the biscuits into melted chocolate to half their width. Wait until the chocolate has hardened, then sandwich together each chocolate-coated half with a plain half, using buttercream made by creaming together the icing sugar and butter. Place each dainty in a paper case.

Makes 18 dainties

Short Paste

1 lb block margarine, 2 lb plain flour
4 oz caster sugar (optional), Cold water

Mix together flour and sugar in a basin (sugar may be omitted if pastry is to be used for savoury dishes, or a mixture of sweet and savoury recipes). Cut margarine into $\frac{1}{2}$ in. cubes, then rub into flour and sugar mixture using the tips of the fingers until the contents of the bowl resembles fine breadcrumbs. Add sufficient cold water, a little at a time, mixing well between each addition, to form a firm dough. Be careful not to add too much water, as this will make the pastry hard and tough. Roll out pastry on a floured board and use as desired — any of the recipes given in this book, which use pastry, are suitable.

To make an **Apple Pie**, *line a pie plate or 1–2 in. deep round tin with pastry (approximately 8 oz of made-up pastry will be needed). Fill case with peeled and sliced apples, piling them up well, or use a tin of apple pie filling. Top with pastry (about 6 oz of made-up pastry will be needed) and bake in a moderate oven, 375°F, 190°C, gas mark 5, for about 45 minutes or until pastry is golden brown and apples are cooked. Sprinkle with caster sugar when cooked, if liked.*

To make **Jam Tarts**, *line the segments of a bun tin with pastry (about 8 oz of made-up pastry will be needed) then place a teaspoon of jam in each case. Place two strips of pastry across the top of each tart, then bake in a moderate oven, 375°F, 190°C, gas mark 5, for about 10 minutes (check to make sure that jam is not burning after 7 minutes) or until pastry is cooked. Cool on a wire rack.*

Wilma Cakes

5 oz margarine, 5 oz caster sugar, 5 oz ground rice
$3\frac{1}{4}$ oz ground almonds, $3\frac{1}{2}$ oz currants, $1\frac{1}{2}$ oz glacé cherries
2 size 3 eggs, Raspberry or strawberry jam
Pastry: 8 oz plain flour, 4 oz margarine

Make pastry using 8 oz flour and 4 oz margarine. Line a deep
swiss roll tin with pastry and spread a little jam evenly over
the base. Cream the margarine and sugar together until light
and fluffy, then add the eggs, one at a time, beating well to
incorporate each egg. Fold in the ground rice, ground almonds,
currants and cherries (chopped into small pieces). Spread this
mixture over the jam in the pastry case. Bake in the centre of a
preheated oven, 350°F, 180°C, gas mark 4, for 35–40 minutes
or until brown. Dust with caster sugar when hot (if liked) and
cut into pieces when cold.

Makes 12 pieces

The Storr Ridge, Skye

The Corrieyairack Pass, Highland

Aberdeen Harbour

Loch Ness, Highland

Edzell Castle, Tayside

The Eildon Hills, Borders